Jarring A Tiny Bird

A Collection of Poems

ALSO BY DALE L. BAKER

More Than I Could Ever Know: How I Survived Caregiving

JARRING A TINY BIRD

A Collection of Poems

by

Dale L. Baker

Peoria, Arizona

ISBN-13: 978-1530352104
ISBN-10: 153035210X

FIRST EDITION
MSDALE PUBLISHING

Manufactured in the United State of America

DEDICATION

To Lulu Woodmansee, my grandmother
who loved me unconditionally from the day I was born,
hung my scrubbed diapers on a frozen clothesline
and cherished every word
I ever wrote her

TABLE OF CONTENTS

Emerald female

Ruby-throated male

. . . how foolish of me

to forget. . .

PICKED FROM AIR

The rounding sounds of words call to me
They float
They glide
They tumble and rumble,
Seducing me to lure them
To set them down in rows
To pair them off
Noun verb, noun verb, noun verb
To spice them with adjectives
To adorn them with festive phrases
To dress them with dangling participles
They laugh at *faux pas*
They giggle at *deja vu*
Those tempting teasing words
I'll never catch them all
They reproduce, recouple and float free
So there are plenty left for you,
And you,
And you,
And you,
As well as for me

MANUSCRIPT ADDICTION

Let me slip into that moment between crisp pages
where strangers like chess pieces play out their lives
line by written line.

On hot cocoa vapors I ride words, saddled in afghan comfort,
composing tragic players who reel against horrors
so wonderfully not mine.

Tethered above chores, let me drift aloft to linger
along streets I will never walk, adventurous trails I will never seek;
to quiver and finger visions of places like so much verbal chiffon.

Too soon, a call, the door, some undivine
intervention splits my cloud, sucking me back to earth.
My euphoric ascension ripped,

solemnly I mark my spot between white sheets
stashing my pen until I can again abuse it,
longing to slip once more into that moment.

POETRY ON ALBERTA STREET

A pub, an open mic, a spotlight, too bright,
in a corner front and center
hopefuls sign up to air their thoughts,
verbalized and prized

Young men salivate tales of skin,
conquest and fruitless hunts
The infirm, complete with canes and limps,
shout out old wounds

Cotton candy spikes, the color of spun sugar
mohawk the head of a leather-clad rapper,
her legs beneath metalicised boots
proclaimed too beautiful to show

Anxious free hands twist an ear, clutch a shoulder,
leverage so the paper-holding hand won't shake,
except for the stool-pounder who takes both fists
to bongo the Naugahyde

Words mist the stage. Raw enthusiasm
showcased in tavern bravado
How many merlots I wonder would it take
to get my name on that list?

THIRTY YEARS TOO LATE FOR THE PARTY

Foot on log, hand on knee; old photograph of me,
Crater Lake and my jeans, same blue hue,
Denim tight, fit so fine, my hair glows like thick honey
What a gorgeous girl I was; sad shame I never knew.

Shyness kept me from the crowds, round shoulders hid my bust.
A desk corralled my hips and thighs, a chair caressed my butt.
I should have been out dancing, luring masculine lust.
Why did I choose to study when I could have been a slut?

HAPPY HOUR

The amber bottle rides to his lips
powered by forearm art,
skin behind the ink
mahogany like the bar
he elbows

From my table
I savor salt and saliva,
my taste buds seeking
taut slick muscle,
to skim each bicep
entwined in tattoo cuffs

Lazily my tongue
chases wine
around the rim of
my glass
chardonnay sheeting slowly
toward stem,
I lick and long for
smooth ridges, glossy pores

Eyes closed, I ponder
pounce now or
forever chew my lip?

HERE TO DANCE

I'm just here to dance
to lap up the lyrics and nuzzle the notes
of others

To slink in black
to slide my tango shoes
along slick parquet
to throbbing *ochos*
my legs returning like magnets
snapping together side by side
only to pivot apart again
with each figure eight.

I'm here to dance
to tap in red
to stamp my salsa heels
flash my fleshy bosom
glistening globes inching higher and higher
bouncing in time to beads bobbing
round my neck

I'm here to dance
I mean dance
tango, salsa, merengue, bachata

Steps with soul
words with fire and flavor
palabras de fuego y sabor
and I'm not surrendering my body

until
I have tired
of
them
all.

CLICKING FOR LOVE

Gals over fifty, yes, point now and click
Online the man of your dreams does exist.
I've sampled eHarmony, joined Match.com
Had lots of laughs, in pursuit of "the one."

I'll save you some time with tips and a tale.
Relax, believe nothing and you won't fail.
"Don't drink alcohol" is code for "in rehab"
"A few pounds extra" means covered with flab

"Divorced" means loser with ex's, all bitches.
Beware of white socks, crew cut, military hitches,
Atheist morticians with time on their hands
"Seeking personal adventure in my own wonderland."

"Young for my age" equals "trolling for sex,
Just bought the pills, want to give them a test."
Also believes his soul mate's eleven
Although he's on oxygen, past eighty-seven.

He'll swear he's a dancer, looking to pair
Then cancel a meeting, confess a wheelchair.
Won't tell you up front about meds and the limp
Just meet him for coffee and follow the hints.

My latest suitor drove in from the coast.
A whole lot older than his picture post
A recent widower, still grieving his loss
Hairless, hopeful, seeking a new boss

He's handy, non-violent, has plenty to say
Can't find much wrong, but who needs "okay?"
Walks, doesn't smoke, seems small town sweet
Not good enough to get this city girl "beached."

A THREE POEM AFFAIR

1. GUILLERMO PRIMERO
(Maui Mornings)

I wake up hungry for you
bird cries mingle with light
cool lanai air settles
on the sheet
that covers us.

Your stillness
draws my fingertips
to touch lightly.

Your smile, opening eyes
invite me
to circle your mouth
with my tongue,

Lingering,
to savor the wetness
measure the passion.

When to dangle my nipples
above your lips,
when to skim them
over your chest

Your hands full of my flesh,
I await the squeeze of your palms
sliding me into place.

We circle
locked
in pelvic embrace.

I wake up hungry for you,
eager to add my cries
to birdsong,
to see pleasure settle
across your face

like cool lanai air,
drifting
over the sheet
that covers us.

2. NOTHING SUBTLE ABOUT WILL (Nothing Left to Love)

In the post-Will pause, I sigh
Able at last to let out the air
To savor my syrah,
Pick at my spinach salad,
Chase chocolate brownie crumbs
Around my gums without guilt or
Timeout for talk or a kiss

I enjoy peace in my special place
Free of pounding jazz,
Floor spills, fashion prompts
From a lover backing away,
Urging me in high volume
To be someone else.

3. GUILLERMO TERMINADO
(My Fill of Will)

I wish you well
But I don't know who you are
The Will I fell in love with
Asked me questions that probed my soul
Listened to my answers
Basked in the smile
Those revelations brought to my face.

My Will filled his day with thoughts of pleasing me.
My Will looked forward to my touch.
I wish you well, stranger, but
You are not my Will.

YOUR MARK ON ME

My soul bears your thumbprint
A permanent crater, casually created
discarded

What good is it now to you?
The heart you carried away
in your pocket

Proclaiming we have nothing
in common.

DRUNK IN THE AFTERNOON

the hole in my heart
like cork pulled from a bottle
a glass tunnel to wine once within

sides so smooth
never together to knit
never to meet

everything
once inside
gone

HOLLOW

You
love me vacantly
the act, not the word.

We
exchange sweat
role-playing between sheets,
imagining, perhaps,
intimacies with others

I
need more than
pelvic passion
and mere moist memories of
desire

PICK UP

There's no room for me inside your head
where fawns lie down with dragons
subdued by your mighty sword.

In my world a mall security guard locks the last door.
Rain splatters my glasses,
drips onto my bag.

When you do descend to earth
hunger will be the driver.
In a dark kitchen
you will notice the lack of cooking smells.

Only then will you focus on
where you left me.

TEDIOUS LOVER

Thick calloused hands
slide over my belly
fingers too thick
and hardened
to find soft spots

My mind floats
moves me
not quick enough
past obligatory touching
focuses on a memory far away

My inner voice
cannot be fooled
or silenced
it screams
I am not a pillow

WATER RITUAL

He has trained me well
to prepare pre-dinner rinse,
disburse excess marinade,
cleanse his finger bowl.

Birdbath keeper, my role
flusher of debris
discarder of soggy bread,
scrubber of concrete.

He watches, clutching gutters
eager to dip, not black shiny feathers,
but, dumpster trophies,
fish heads, bones of fowl.

Brazen crow, bobs at my roof's edge
chiding me to hurry, anxious
to dowse another serving
resume a meal that has no end.

I fetch the hose, curse,
comply.

GOOD-BYE, GIRLFRIEND

Your friendship, like a rock under my toe
troublesome, yet familiar over time,
kicked up and lodged decades ago
along some crowded footpath.

Often I thought to extract it from my shoe
discouraged by the chore of unlacing,
purging, re-tying
and time lost forever in the task.

Enduring blister, callus, thickening against
your unpleasantries, I weighed pros, cons.
Scales accumulated a grain of sand
each time to the negative balance.

Mercifully, a tipping point,
routine irritation
grown boulder wide,
halted my plodding.

Your friendship dropped easily where it fell
rolled into the grass, far from the trail.
Lightened by the load, my arches flexed,
my soles eager to feel higher ground.

JEWELRY MAGIC

It glistened under glass
Too expensive to suffer
The touch of frivolous buyers
The chain twinkled
The red charm begged to be held
It beckoned me to liberate it
From its padded showcase
To fasten it around my neck
The crafted heart to settle in my cleavage
To rise and fall there with my breath
To cling to beads of perspiration
To settle and lodge against my heart

THE FOLKS

Sister, I ask
When did it happen?
That line crossed,
Where was it?
When did our titanic parents
deflate into
dottering old people
we laugh at?

ONE SIDED MEMORIES

You don't remember
but
the bus would
leave you standing
across the street
I would wait
on the corner
so you could hold my hand
We walked home
together
I was 4
You were Daddy

My plane would circle
I saw you standing
sunny, open-air
airport courtyard
your baby-blue, beat-up floppy hat
a beacon to me from my window seat
the plane circling
bringing me home
my first college break
I was 19
You were Dad

At the airport
that last time
after Mom's stroke
you waited for me
I saw you
I was 50
You were ancient

You sobbed in the kitchen
an unforgettable sob
the phone still in your hand
ceiling light glistening off
silver strands atop
your baby pink scalp
Mom wasn't coming home

You never remembered
much of anything
after that

MOM'S LAST WINTER

Careful not to tug or pinch
I snap her into her coat
As if she were a toddler,
Fish her sleeves for rumpled sweater
Coax cap over ears
Fetch her walker from behind the door.

Her head, my chin,
No longer eye to eye.

When I was the toddler
When she buttoned my snowsuit,
Warm worn hands
Brushing the flesh of my face,
Preparing me for a journey
In tow, again, at her side,

Did she ever feel this weary?
Ever dread the spring?

ROOM 134A

It takes two people
One on each side
To lift Dad

From wheelchair to bed
From bed to wheelchair
From wheelchair to commode

To bed
To commode
To wheelchair
It takes two people.

Dad will die here
Room 134A
Lifted daily by
Two people

Other people
Not Mom
Not me

AIMLESS

Mom cussed and tossed insults.
Dad stayed put inside the *Wall Street Journal.*

For decades,
fear of going home
drove me forward,
seeking, succeeding,
pressing on.

They're both gone now and
I find I don't belong anywhere.

BEYOND THE PROM

Shadowed figures slide over polished wood
Paired silhouettes cling to shared lyrics, secret sounds.

Through glass and time, I strain to feel the rhythm.
Silence consumes my search.

My ears seek music.
I long to feel the magic of their movement.

Adrift among toneless decades, never to join in,
I imagine them slow-dancing still.

Concurrent journeys straddle a window draped in memory
I want to trade my shipwreck for their voyage.

NO MORE DUETS

You fight for breath
no match for that
hungry mass
squeezing
your sighs

My breath responds
clings inside my lungs
lingers
I cannot focus on
how to push
air out

Your body, mine
one shared chord
together
we surrender
two-voice harmony

together
we submit
to one
solidified
song.

Silently now,
we are three,
Cancer, you
and me.

A CAREGIVER'S DAYDREAM

To escape this moment, this here, this now
I launch dreams forward or exhausted, drift back.
So hard to dwell here, where we are.

Today presses like a sharp-edged cookie cutter,
Outlining two sets of limbs rolled flat and stuck
in temporal goo.
Your life dissolves by dollops,
I mourn each plop, each loss.

This here and now, a time we did not request
I wait for it to pass, this moment I'll forget.
Like memories strained through cheesecloth
I'll remember pieces.

CONVERSATIONAL OUTCAST

Oh, how is he doing? they ask with eyes
scanning the room for better options.
My response, no matter its content
will end the talk.

They have already moved on
to brighter subjects . . . *the best time for planting basil. . .*
last night's interview with. . .
before I part my lips.

Once or twice, at first,
I took the query at face value,
an honest interest in my circumstances.
He's on hospice now. . .

They've switched his pain meds . . .
but quickly I was left standing alone
so I abbreviate.
He's fine.

It has not helped. They are
aware of my inability
to have anything of interest
to say. I reside in

that category of
Poor Thing.
Too bad about her husband . . .
Did you see the price of gas . . .?

FADE TO NIGHT

Twilight moments replace CT's and chemo.
Beyond the anger, past the denial,
we are now here,
enjoying this bridge to the unknown,
savoring each hour, yearning for another verdict,
but expecting no miracle.

We have been we for decades.
Now, this sundown, the end of us as a pair,
feathers soft blues and whites into golden pinks,
stretching on earth a horizontal grin from ear to ear.

Our togetherness is on the horizon,
a slow motion sunset, slipping into unimagined color,
unanticipated calm,
a sundown collapsing like bleeding watercolors
into black.

Too soon, that unknown eventual dawn will find us,
that inescapable morning when we emerge
to separate lonelinesses,
a dimension apart.

But today, hummingbirds buzz combat over sugar water,
flickers and bushtits attack suets cakes.
We devour sweet salmon dinner,
popcorn, watch the World Series for dessert.

We relish our warm, glowing sunset,
cold night, a distant given.

WARLORD OF THE PATIO ON 27TH STREET

Magenta would be an awkward name, so we just call him Red,
not his wing and breast tone, but the color of his head.
His helmet, black in shadow, is crimson in the sun,
a fiery backyard dynamo, his job is never done.

Rival hummers test his skill, their tongues will touch the prize,
but Red attacks to end the drink and vault them through the skies.
Owner of the feeder, he's the sugar syrup king.
Red patrols, defeats the foes and settles down to sing.

His head thrown back, his throat swells wide, he sways like Stevie Wonder.
Too bad his song, unbirdlike, is just metallic stutter,
Like a spring about to snap, wound tight, an ugly clatter,
a whirling, straining, grinding noise, a sound more like a chatter.

He's got the looks. He's got the buzz. Shame he's not a singer.
But Red's a hit show every day as he defends his dinner.
We never lack for intrigue from our deck-chair front-row seats.
Bravo, patio warlord of 27th Street!

LOVE BIRDS

They sat on either side of
sugar water,
Emerald female
Ruby-throated male.

Through our kitchen window,
I watched,
waiting for them
to squabble and bolt.

When they lingered
I smiled.
Swaying together, they sipped
separated by glass.

I knew you'd be thrilled when I told you,
disappointed that you were not here.
Then
I remembered.

What's left of you fills an urn
in the living room.

You've seen your last hummingbird,
enjoyed your last
magnolia-shaded summer
beneath
pint-sized buzz.

How foolish of me
To forget.

MAKING MY HARP SING

Notes congregate at the small of my back
dots, flags, hollow circles and black bubbles
quickened by each measure
they swell with excitement
compressed and alive they clamber
taking proper place
in line

Breaching my marrow
flooding past my elbows
vibrating in time like rhythmic lava rushing
seeking to spill out
through fingertips and thumbs
that hammer rapid fire
daring taut strings
to snap

The melody pounds in my ears
a steady companion voice rides it
like a surfing wave
only the heaving of my chest
tells me
it's mine

HOMECOMING

I lost myself
somewhere
unrecognizable among
affairs of others

bumped and dislodged by
overflowing adjacent lives
spreading their needs
three inches thick
all over me

Unaware of my loss
I stumbled across me
and then
Like an old friend
I startled myself,
Oh hi . . . I've missed you

Snuggling me
with the warmth
of a comforter under my chin
Peace reclaimed me.
I wanted to feel this good always.
I am who I have always been.

BEAUTIFUL WOMAN

If only I had known I was a beautiful child
No one ever told me
Not a hint
Not a single word was said
So I continued my role, trudging along
As a two-headed, wart-covered toad
Until I tripped over a mirror
and broke
into a smile

GPS VOICES INSIDE MY HEAD

My right brain loves French fries and fudge,
My left brain chides me for my growing pudge,
Right side flings me with abandon onto the floor
to dance every beat,
Left side flashes *Idiot! Remember you have scoliosis and flat feet,*
Right delights in licks of gelato,
Left braces for cramps and diarrhea that follow,
Right savors sips of chardonnay,
Left screams, *Cirrhosis can't be far away,*
Right keeps me up for days writing the world's greatest haiku,
Left reminds me poetry doesn't pay
The bills
Bi-polar?
Schizophrenic?
Am I headed down that splintered road?
Left brain mechanically drones,
You have reached your destination.
But I know
Beyond the monotone noise
Just one crimson brush stroke away
Destination is on my right.

DELICIOUSLY OUT OF TOUCH

Make-believe
repeatedly soiled by reality
plays in my room
revived by chocolate.
Dreams dance
one person strong
one soul deep.

DIMINISHED

I thought I had been here before.
That mole on my neck that turned ugly.
The dimple on my left breast
just below the nipple.
The shadow on my chest x-ray.
Close-calls don't matter now.

My doctor sits on a padded stool, my file
splayed open like a girlie magazine on his desk,
his lips, like the wheels on his stool moving,
making noise. My mind stuck on "cancer"
and "tumors" with an 's.'

The exam room echoes the scratch of his pen.
The hand at the end of a white sleeve scribbles
chart notes, a referral, a piece of paper
placed in my hand.

My ticket to the end of my life,
admission to a world of chemicals and toxic procedures
so invasive I cannot grasp their horror.

I know only that his stool has four casters,
he is left-handed

and my voice is too small

MY BACKYARD MEMORIAL SERVICE

She loved to laugh they'll say,
my circle of friends
reliving jovial accounts of my antics,
an ordinary life reframed with humor.

And what a gardener they'll brag.
Talented in so many ways they'll agree,
awed by the discovery of my brush strokes,
brash colors on canvas left behind.

They'll delight in my dance trophies,
faded watercolors, half-completed sculptures,
as if knowing me equaled membership in
a coveted artistic club.

Too bad she couldn't sing.
An awkward silence will follow.
The one who said it will wrestle with guilt,
the others recalling cacophony.

No wonder she kept laughing,
someone will surmise.
Lifting glasses on my patio
all will guffaw.

The echo of their laughter
will jar an adjacent bird,
hovering him above the lavender face
of my favorite hibiscus.

A SIXTY-NINE-YEAR-OLD 69ER

It is January 2016
I am 69
69
69
69
A 6 and a 9
It has a certain
symmetry
The 6 becomes the 9
A roundness
you can flip it
twirl it
set it on its side
still the number
reads the same
its meaning will not change
I am
69
years old
and counting

THANK YOU, MRS. PARRISH

Her gnarled knuckles clutched chalk stubs
stiff hips moved left to right, obscuring
the blackboard's message soon to emerge,
she silenced us with anticipation

Sixth-graders in rows, we longed for her assignments
loved her teaching magic, oblivious to its enduring value,
her arthritic fingers outstretched to us all
we lifted eager hands higher, further

My hand reached for the sky
more thirsty for life than Adam's body
reclining across the Sistine Chapel's ceiling
merely waiting for God's touch

My hand strained to please her
that limping woman in open-toed shoes,
I reached higher, further until
her chalky fingertip ignited mine

I received the gift of expression
a lust for language appeased
only by a steady flow of words

Anointed by chalk dust,
in a rigid classroom seat,
I began to write

WHY POETRY

words come to me
silver threads that
weave in and out of life

like bronze shimmering strings
they pierce muddy brown and
dreary blue routines

these metallic moments
twinkle into my eyes
catch me
unaware
render insignificant the abundant greys
that would choke
vitality from my daily tapestry

I write vibrant verbal color
passions that pull
the fabric of my life
together
give it form
make it whole
make it worthy to be worn
and
now and then
wickedly unfurled

ACKNOWLEDGEMENTS

Dale L. Baker wishes to acknowledge the following poems included in this collection appeared individually sometimes in earlier versions in the following publications:

"Picked From Air"
"Thirty Years Too Late For the Party"
"Here to Dance"
Maui Muses, Vol 4, Equitude 2015

"Manuscript Addiction"
May/June 2008 issue *Writer's Journal*

"Room 134A"
Toe Good Poetry 2011 online magazine

"Fade To Night"
November/December 2005 issue *Today's Caregiver*

"Diminished"
VoiceCatcher 3, 2008 anthology

"My Backyard Memorial Service"
Take a Bite of Literature, 2009 collection of work distributed to customers of The Bite Restaurant in Rockaway Beach and anthology later printed by Oregon Writers Colony.

ABOUT THE POET

DALE L. BAKER was born in New Vienna, Ohio. Her first book, a memoir, *More Than I Could Ever Know: How I Survived Caregiving* won a Bronze Medal in the 2014 Living Now Book Awards, was a Finalist in the 2014 USA Best Book Awards and placed as a Red Ribbon Winner in the 2014 Wishing Shelf Book Awards. A graduate of Lewis & Clark College and retired civil servant Ms. Dale enjoys reading her poetry at public events in Arizona and Hawaii.

http://www.msdaleLbaker.com

http://www.amazon.com/Ms-Dale-L.-Baker

Made in the USA
Las Vegas, NV
09 March 2022